Claude Wenzler

THE KINGS OF FRANCE

Translated by : Angela Moyon

ÉDITIONS OUEST-FRANCE
13 rue du Breil, Rennes

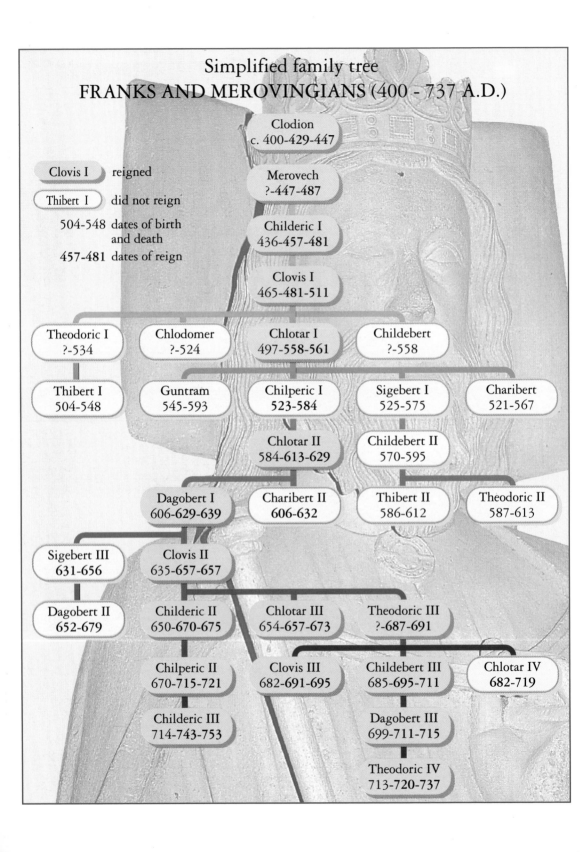

Simplified family tree
FRANKS AND MEROVINGIANS (400 - 737 A.D.)

Clodion
c. 400-429-447

Clovis I — reigned

Thibert I — did not reign

504-548 dates of birth and death
457-481 dates of reign

Merovech
?-447-487

Childeric I
436-457-481

Clovis I
465-481-511

Theodoric I
?-534

Chlodomer
?-524

Chlotar I
497-558-561

Childebert
?-558

Thibert I
504-548

Guntram
545-593

Chilperic I
523-584

Sigebert I
525-575

Charibert
521-567

Chlotar II
584-613-629

Childebert II
570-595

Dagobert I
606-629-639

Charibert II
606-632

Thibert II
586-612

Theodoric II
587-613

Sigebert III
631-656

Clovis II
635-657-657

Dagobert II
652-679

Childeric II
650-670-675

Chlotar III
654-657-673

Theodoric III
?-687-691

Chilperic II
670-715-721

Clovis III
682-691-695

Childebert III
685-695-711

Chlotar IV
682-719

Childeric III
714-743-753

Dagobert III
699-711-715

Theodoric IV
713-720-737

The Great Dynasties

The Franks

The Franks can be divided into two main families. The largest of the two groups formed the Salian Franks who had their own law, the «Lex Saliqua», a strictly formalist procedure handed down by word of mouth and based on a system of compensation for the victims of violence or personal injury. The other group consisted of the Rhineland Franks who lived on the banks of the Rhine and Moselle rivers.

The Franks first appeared in the history books in the mid 3rd Century, proving to be redoubtable enemies when attacking from the sea during pirate raids along the coast of the North Sea, and on land during incursions into Gaul in 258 A.D. After conquering the country in the 5th and 6th Centuries, the Germanic tribe imposed its name on Gaul.

The Frankish conquest was, initially at least, peaceful. There were Franks among the Roman legionaries where they were employed as auxiliaries or, in some cases, high-ranking officers. One such was Merobaud, who was appointed Magister Peditum, i.e. General, by Emperor Valentinian in 375 A.D. Other Franks settled right across the Roman Empire, colonising entire areas.

After the Barbarian invasions of 406 A.D, Rome's authority went into a decline and the Franks took advantage of the situation to extend their power, gradually. Chlodion, the founder of the Merovingian dynasty, conquered the north of Gaul as far as the Somme after capturing Cambrai (c. 430-440 A.D.) while the Rhenish Franks occupied what is now known as Rhineland.

The advance of the Franks was slow until the 5th Century when Clovis brought all the Gallic tribes under his authority.

The Merovingians

Initially, in the 5th Century, the dynasty ruled over the Salian Franks; later, as a result of Clovis' conquests, it extended its supremacy right across Gaul until Pepin the Short took power in 751 A.D.

Although Pharamond, a Frankish chieftain who died in 428 and was a distant forebear of Clovis, is known to have existed, the Merovingian dynasty entered the history books slowly and discreetly, with Chlodion the Hairy who became King of Cambrai after capturing Northern Gaul (c. 430-440 A.D.). He was followed by Merovech who gave his name to the first dynasty of Kings of France and who helped the Roman General Aetius to defeat Attila the Hun at the Battle of the Catalaunian Plains in 451 A.D. He was followed by Childeric I, said to be Merovech' son, who was King of Tournai.

It is, though, Clovis I, Childeric I's son, who is considered as the founder of the dynasty, both for his energetic struggle to unite the various Frankish peoples and for his domination of much of Gaul.

Urged by Clotilda, a Burgundian princess whom he had taken as his wife, he was christened, with three thousand of his soldiers, in Reims in 496 A.D. He was the only Barbarian King to have espoused the Christian religion and, thereafter, Clovis enjoyed the support of the Church.

After his death in 511 A.D, his conquests were divided between his four sons - Theodoric I, Chlodomer, Childebert I and Chlotar I, all of whom continued his expansionist policies by annexing the kingdom of Burgundy (534 A.D.) and acquiring Provence (537 A.D.).

After overcoming rivalries, escaping a number of attempts on his life, and taking advantage of the deaths of his brothers, Chlotar succeeded in re-establishing the unity of the Regnum Francorum in 558 A.D. His own death in 561 A.D, however, led to further division of the kingdom between his sons. Charibert became King of Paris (561-567 A.D.), Guntram became King of Burgundy (561-593 A.D.), Sigebert inherited Austrasia (561-575 A.D.) and Chilperic I was given the kingdom of Soissons (561-584 A.D.). This division led to new rivalries and bloody conflict.

Simplified family tree
CAROLINGIANS
(715 - 987 A.D.)

Pepin the Elder
c. 580-640

Ansegisel
?-679

Pepin of Heristal
c. 640-714

Charles Martel
685-741

Pepin the Short
715-**751-768**

Charlemagne
742-**768-814**

Carloman
751-**768-771**

Charles
?-813

Louis the Pious
778-**814-840**

Pepin
806-810

Louis the German
804-843

Charles II
823-**840-877**

Charles the Fat
839-**884-888**

Louis II
846-**877-879**

Carloman
866-**879-884**

Louis III
863-**879-882**

Charles III
879-**898-929**

Louis IV
918-**936-954**

806-810   dates of birth
              and death

806-810 dates of reign

Louis II   reigned

Pepin   did not reign

Lothair
941-**954-986**

Louis V
967-**986-987**

Dagobert's monarchy was strong and stable but the reigns of his sons, Sigebert III, King of Austrasia, and Clovis II, King of Burgundy and Neustria, were marked by a return to strife and the handing over of power to the noblemen including the mayors of the palace.

So it was that, from 679 A.D. onwards, the power and authority of Pepin of Héristal, mayor of the palace, began to become apparent. From then on, during the reigns of the so-called «lazy» monarchs (Clovis III, Childebert III, Dagobert III, Chilperic II, Chlotar IV and Theodoric IV), Pepin and his descendents governed the entire Regnum Francorium. Taking advantage of this hold on power, and supported by a strong network of loyalties, Pepin the Short had the last Merovingian monarch, Childeric III, confined to a monastery with the agreement of Pope Zacharias. He then seized the royal title in 751 A.D.

The Carolingians

This Frankish family was directly descended from the Pepinides (named after Pepin of Landen, the grandfather of Pepin of Héristal) and it gradually took over power from the decadent Merovingians. Pepin the Short, Charles Martel's son, seized royal power in 751 A.D. with the support of the Pope, St. Boniface, who crowned him in Soissons in 752 A.D. This alliance between the monarchy and the Church gave the Carolingians even greater power. Pepin the Short and Charlemagne, who defended the Pope's interests in Italy, engaged in an active expansionist policy designed to extend both the Regnum Francorum and Christianity itself. The religion was carried to the banks of the Elbe.

Territorial expansion began c. 755 A.D. when Pepin the Short responded to a call for assistance from Pope Stephen II, who was under threat from the Lombards, and it continued with Pepin's son, Charles, who intervened in Italy to conquer the kingdom of Lombardy, in Germany and in Spain. It was more or less complete by the end of the 8th Century and it strengthened Charles' prestige. As the sole holder of temporal authority throughout the Christian world, he was crowned «Emperor of the Holy Roman Empire» in Rome in the year 800 A.D. by Pope Leo III, thereby giving even greater substance to the union between Empire and Papacy.

The Empire reached the peak of its might during the reign of Charlemagne but its power was, in some respects, mere illusion. Given the many States within the Empire, its unity was closely dependent on the personality and character of the man at its head. If, as was the case with Charlemagne, its leader was powerful, the Empire was strong; if its leader showed any sign of weakness (as did Louis I the Pious), the Empire was more fragile and less secure, especially as the Frankish law of subdivision of inherited property still remained in force.

Thus it was that, in 806 A.D, Charlemagne made provision for the division of his empire between his three sons under the Deed of Thionville but Pepin's death in 810 A.D, followed by Charles' death in 813, left Louis I the Pious sole heir to the throne. However, Louis granted his share of the inheritance to his son, Charles the Bald, thereby causing a dynastic quarrel that was to mark the downfall of the Empire. His deed of inheritance went against the Ordinatio Imperii signed in 817 A.D. which acknowledged Lothair to be the sole heir to the imperial throne.

Louis I's reign was then marked by rebellions on the part of his sons Lothair, Pepin and Louis the German. These dynastic rivalries continued after his death, eventually leading to the Treaty of Verdun in 843 A.D, under the terms of which the Empire was divided into three kingdoms attributed to Lothair, Louis the German and Charles the Bald.

The weakness of this dynasty was its style of government. The country was ineffectually administered, power lay in the hands of family and friends, and the Emperor's orders were passed on by word of mouth. This encouraged the spread of a powerful feudal system and, at the same time, the territorial apportionment that followed each death led to a division of kingdoms and, in the final event, to the disintegration of the Western World.

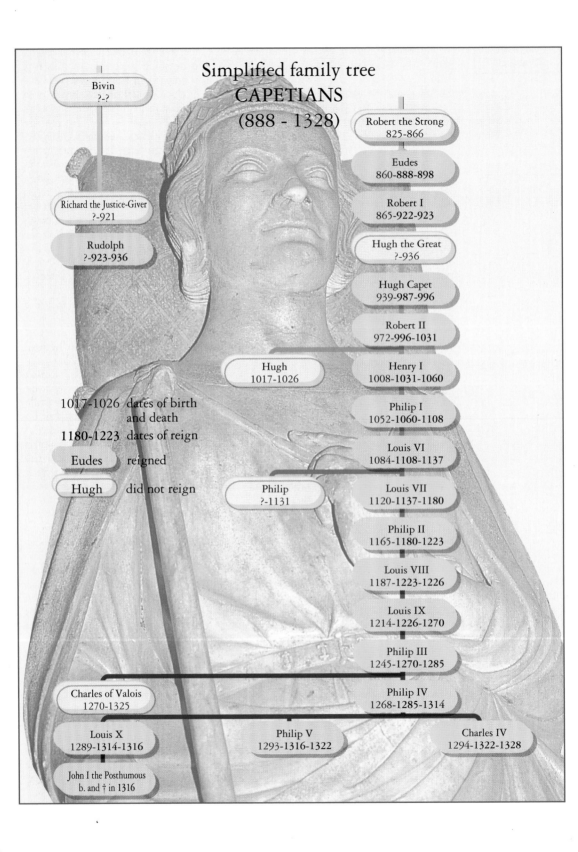

Simplified family tree
CAPETIANS
(888 - 1328)

Bivin
?-?

Robert the Strong
825-866

Eudes
860-**888-898**

Richard the Justice-Giver
?-921

Robert I
865-**922-923**

Rudolph
?-**923-936**

Hugh the Great
?-936

Hugh Capet
939-**987-996**

Robert II
972-**996-1031**

Hugh
1017-1026

Henry I
1008-**1031-1060**

1017-1026 dates of birth
and death

1180-1223 dates of reign

Eudes reigned

Hugh did not reign

Philip I
1052-**1060-1108**

Louis VI
1084-**1108-1137**

Philip
?-1131

Louis VII
1120-**1137-1180**

Philip II
1165-**1180-1223**

Louis VIII
1187-**1223-1226**

Louis IX
1214-**1226-1270**

Philip III
1245-**1270-1285**

Charles of Valois
1270-1325

Philip IV
1268-**1285-1314**

Louis X
1289-**1314-1316**

Philip V
1293-**1316-1322**

Charles IV
1294-**1322-1328**

John I the Posthumous
b. and † in 1316

The Capetians

This dynasty, which reigned from 987 A.D. to 1328, owes its name to Hugh Capet whose family played a major role in the political arena from the days of Robert the Strong onwards. It was after the death of the last Carolingian monarch, Louis V, that Hugh Capet mounted the throne and, by doing so, marked the real beginnings of the House of Capet. Masters, in 987 A.D, of a modest estate in the Paris Basin surrounded on all sides by lands belonging to leading noblemen of the day, the Capetians worked hard to expand their territory and exercise direct authority over it. They were the veritable founders of royal power in France.

Like the great feudal lords of the realm, Hugh Capet, who died in 996 A.D, and his descendents of the direct line (Robert II, Henry I, Philip I) played a role that was initially discreet. Yet the Capets proved particularly skilful in taking advantage of certain customs. Thus it was that, in the early years of the dynasty, the principle of an elected monarch was upheld. This explained why kings guaranteed their succession to the throne by involving their eldest sons in government, thereby ensuring that, in most cases, they would succeed their fathers to the throne. Gradually, however, the Capetians succeeded in imposing the rule of heredity. Royal authority, strengthened by the hereditary claim to the monarchy, was also reinforced by the coronation ceremony, through which the king was vested with a divine mission.

In the 12th Century, Louis the Fat and Louis VII did their utmost, in a subtle manner, to reinforce the authority and power of the monarchy, by using their feudal prerogatives as sovereigns. Homage was paid to each new king at his coronation. This created personal links, man-to-man relationships through which the vassals placed their trust in the king and assured him of their loyalty. Moreover, the Capetians accustomed the leading feudal lords to see the monarchy as a force to be reckoned with by frequently intervening on their lands.

The use of feudal rights spread, in fact, as a result of the expansion of the royal estates, which were extended through marriages, joint ownership agreements, purchases or conquests. Philip Augustus even succeeded in removing the vast enclave that was the Plantagenet domaine in the provinces of Western France (the struggle against the English remained one of the priorities throughout the reign of the Capetian dynasty). The Crown estates underwent remarkable expansion. On the death of the last Capetian monarch, Charles IV the Fair, in 1328, only Flanders, Brittany and Burgundy remained outside a kingdom whose borders more or less followed the meanders of the Scheldt, Meuse and Rhône.

An expansionist policy of this size required an efficient administrative body. The Capetian monarchs therefore created new institutions such as the King's Counsel, the royal law courts, the Chamber of Accounts etc. all of which enabled the kingdom to gradually shake off the feudal system and exist as a State while the sovereign extended his power to all his subjects.

When Charles IV the Fair died without leaving a male heir, the Crown did not pass to Isabella, daughter of Philip IV the Fair because of the Salic law which excluded women from succeeding to the throne; instead, it passed to his cousin, Philip VI of Valois.

The Valois

This House, which governed France from 1328 to 1589, had three branches:

• The direct line descended from Charles of Valois, younger brother of Philip IV the Fair. The family reigned from Philip VI's accession to the throne in 1328 until the death, without an heir, of Charles VIII in 1498.

• The Valois-Orléans branch, who were descended from Louis I d'Orléans, second son of Charles V, and who mounted the throne in 1498, with the accession of Louis XII.

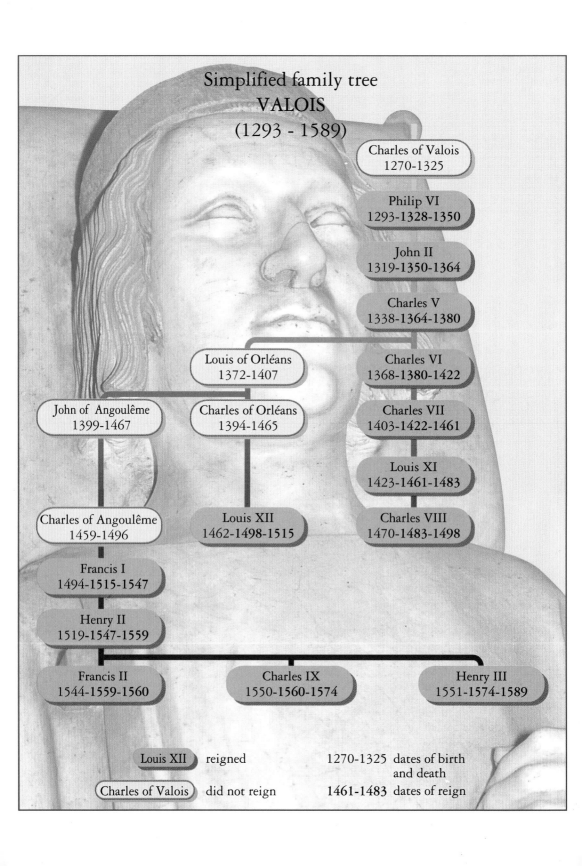

Simplified family tree
VALOIS
(1293 - 1589)

Charles of Valois
1270-1325

Philip VI
1293-1328-1350

John II
1319-1350-1364

Charles V
1338-1364-1380

Louis of Orléans
1372-1407

Charles VI
1368-1380-1422

John of Angoulême
1399-1467

Charles of Orléans
1394-1465

Charles VII
1403-1422-1461

Louis XI
1423-1461-1483

Charles of Angoulême
1459-1496

Louis XII
1462-1498-1515

Charles VIII
1470-1483-1498

Francis I
1494-1515-1547

Henry II
1519-1547-1559

Francis II
1544-1559-1560

Charles IX
1550-1560-1574

Henry III
1551-1574-1589

Louis XII — reigned   1270-1325 dates of birth and death

Charles of Valois — did not reign   1461-1483 dates of reign

• The Valois-Angoulême branch, who were descended from Louis I d'Angoulême and who acceded to the throne on the death of Louis XII, with Francis I in 1515. They retained the monarchy until Henry III died without an heir, in 1589.

As soon as the House of Valois mounted the throne, it was confronted with the difficulties arising from the One Hundred Years' War. Its authority was then weakened by defeat and by the English occupation of part of the kingdom, while its sovereignty, which was contested by feudal lords whose lands had been granted to them in appanage, was threatened by the division of the country into supporters of the Armagnacs and supporters of the Burgundians.

Joan of Arc's legendary and epic journey, however, was to revive the flagging House of Valois and bring back a feeling of patriotism which enabled Charles VII to push the English invaders back across the country's borders.

The last two Valois sovereigns (Charles VII and Louis XI) saw the monarchy as an institution based on divine right, drawing its strength from the concept of absolute power. They imposed their will on the great feudal lords and, by perfecting the country's institutions, completed the centralisation of authority and power.

The Bourbons

It was in the 13th Century that the fourth House of Bourbon was founded. It got its name from Bourbon-l'Archambault, capital of the Duchy of Bourbon. Its founder was Robert, Comte de Clermont, who died in 1317. He was the sixth son of St. Louis and the husband of Béatrice de Bourbon. Two main branches descended from this House - the senior line and the junior line of La Marche-Vendôme.

Descended from Pierre I (1311-1356), the senior branch gave to France Pierre II, Seigneur de Beaujeu, seventh Duke of Bourbon and husband of Anne of France with whom he exercised joint power as co-regent until Charles VIII came of age.

There was also Charles III, eighth Duke of Bourbon, Constable of France, who was dispossessed of his duchy in 1523 by Francis I because he had associated with the Holy Roman Emperor Charles V. His duchy was then given to the House of Marche-Vendôme represented by Antoine of Bourbon, who died in 1562. He was the husband of Jeanne d'Albret and the father of Henry of Navarre, the future Henry IV... The House of Marche-Vendôme was to reign over France in an almost continuous line from 1589 to 1830, with Henry IV, Louis XIII, Louis XIV, Louis XV, Louis XVI, Louis XVIII, and Charles X. The line died out in 1883 with the death, childless, of the Count of Chambord in Frohsdorf.

Numerous lines descended from the Bourbon-Vendôme branch:

• The Condés: Descendents of Louis I of Bourbon, Prince de Condé, and more generally thought of in terms of The Great Condé, this line died out in 1804 on the death of the Duke d'Enghien. It gave rise to the Contis, a branch which died out in 1814.

• The two branches of the Bourbon-Orléans family: The first branch consisted solely of Gaston d'Orléans (d. 1660), brother of Louis XIII and father of the Great Mademoiselle who died childless in 1693. The second branch, which was descended from Philip, Duke d'Orléans, brother of Louis XIV, reigned through Louis-Philippe. At present, it is represented by the Count of Paris, who was born in 1908.

• The Spanish Bourbons: The family acceded to the throne of Spain in 1700 with Philip V, Duke d'Anjou, third grandson of Louis XIV, who died in 1745. Juan Carlos, grandson of Alfonso XIII, who was proclaimed King of Spain in 1975 after the death of General Franco, descends in a direct line from Philip V. Various branches were descended from the Spanish Bourbons including the Parmesan-Bourbons, from Philip the younger son of Philip V, Duke of Parma, who lost the Duchy of Parma in 1860. There were also the Neapolitan-Sicilian Bourbons, descended from Ferdinand, second son of Charles III of Spain, King of the Two Sicilies. This family was also dispossessed of its lands in 1860.

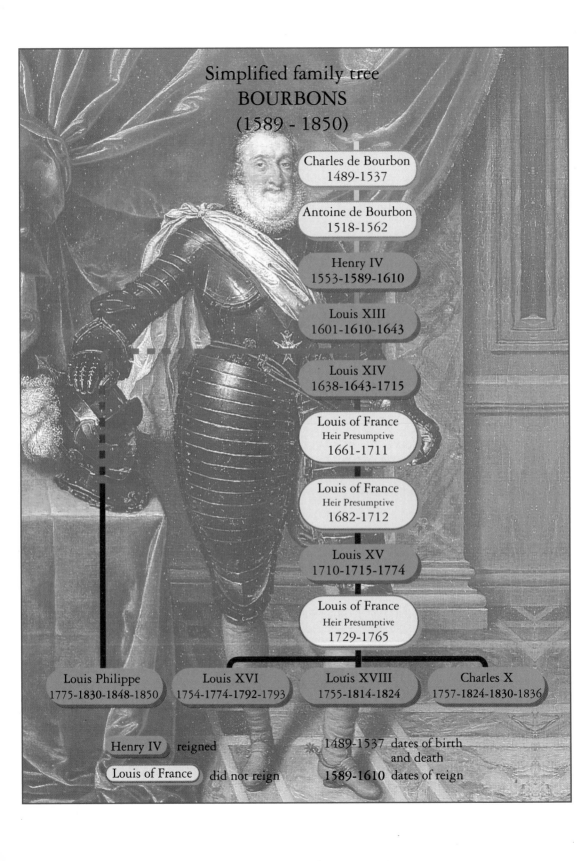

Simplified family tree
BOURBONS
(1589 - 1850)

Charles de Bourbon
1489-1537

Antoine de Bourbon
1518-1562

Henry IV
1553-1589-1610

Louis XIII
1601-1610-1643

Louis XIV
1638-1643-1715

Louis of France
Heir Presumptive
1661-1711

Louis of France
Heir Presumptive
1682-1712

Louis XV
1710-1715-1774

Louis of France
Heir Presumptive
1729-1765

Louis Philippe
1775-1830-1848-1850

Louis XVI
1754-1774-1792-1793

Louis XVIII
1755-1814-1824

Charles X
1757-1824-1830-1836

Henry IV   reigned   1489-1537   dates of birth
                                                   and death

Louis of France   did not reign   1589-1610   dates of reign

Kings of France

The Franks

CHLODION THE HAIRY
c. 400 - 429 - 447 A.D.

Chlodion was a Frankish chieftain who ruled the Salian Franks from 429 A.D. until his death in 447. His reign marked the beginning of the Merovingian Era.

MEROVECH
? - 447 - 457 A.D.

Thought to be the son of Chlodion. He succeeded him in 447 A.D.

CHILDERIC I
436 - 457 - 481 A.D.
Queen: Basine, ? - 463 - ?

The last of the pagan kings. He succeeded his father, Merovech, in 457 A.D.

The Merovingians

CLOVIS
465 - 481 - Paris 511 A.D.
Queen: Clotilda, 475 - 493 - 545 A.D.

Son of Childeric I and Basine, Clovis gradually extended his authority over almost all the tribes of Gaul. In 486 A.D, he defeated Syagrius, the last Roman ruler in Gaul, then conquered Gontebaud, King of the Burgundians, in 500 A.D. near Dijon and Alaric II, King of the Visigoths, in 507 A.D. in Vouillé... Urged by his wife, Clotilda, he was baptised into the Christian faith in Reims on Christmas Day 496 A.D. by St. Remigius. He was the only Barbarian king to have espoused the Roman Catholic religion and, thereafter, Clovis was supported by the Church. In accordance with the Frankish laws of succession, his kingdom was divided between his four sons after his death.

CHLOTAR I THE ELDER
497 - 558 - Compiègne 561 A.D.
Queen: Radegunda, 519 - 538 - 587 A.D.

Chlotar was Clovis' youngest son and he had to reconquer the lands belonging to his brothers. On his death, the kingdom was again divided between his four sons.

CHLOTAR II THE YOUNGER
584 - 613 - 629
Queen: Bertrude, , - ? - 620 A.D.

Son of Chilperic I (523 - 584 A.D.) and Fredegund, he was king of the Franks from 613 to 629 A.D.

DAGOBERT I
605 - 629 - 639
Queen: Nantilda, 610 - 629 - 642 A.D.

Dagobert was the son of Chlotar II and Bertrude, and was designated King during the lifetime of his father c. 623 A.D. He was placed under the guardianship of Pepin of Landen. Surrounded by enlightened counsellors (St. Ouen and St. Ely), he re-established the unity of the «Regnum Francorum» and restored royal authority.

CLOVIS II
635 - 657 - 657 A.D.
Queen: Bathilda, ? - 651 - 680 A.D.

Having become king of almost the entire country in 657 A.D, he left his mother and the mayors of the palace to govern in his place.

CHLOTAR III
654 - 657 - 673 A.D.

Eldest son of Clovis II and Bathilda. He left the mayor of the palace to govern in his place.

CHILDERIC II
650 - 670 - 675 A.D.

Second son of Clovis II. He, too, left the mayor of the palace to hold the reins of government. He was murdered during a hunt in Bondy Forest.

THEODORIC III
654 - 687 - 695 A.D.
Queen: Clothilda - ? - 675 - 691 A.D.

His reign was troubled by internecine struggles and rivalry between those seeking to hold power. The mayors of the palace intervened frequently.

CLOVIS III
682 - 691 - 695 A.D.
Queen: Tanaquille, ? - ? - 696 A.D.

Recumbent statues in the basilica church of Saint-Denis.

Left to right and top to bottom:
Clovis I,
Dagobert I,
Clovis II,
Pepin the Short.
(Photos by Hervé Champollion)

Son of Theodoric III and Clothilda, he reigned in name only; power lay in the hands of Pepin of Heristal. He died without leaving an heir.

CHILDEBERT III
683 - 695 - 711 A.D.
Queen: Edonne, ? - ? - ?

Childebert was one of Theodoric III's sons. He was totally dominated by the mayor of the palace, Pepin of Heristal, to whom he delegated all power. He was the supreme example of a «lazy king».

DAGOBERT III
699 - 711 - 715 A.D.

Son of Childebert III, he left Pepin of Heristal to govern in his name.

CHILPERIC II
670 - 715 - 721 A.D.

Son of Childeric II, he was initially protected by his mayor of the palace, Charles Martel. However, Martel abandoned him and acknowledged Chlotar IV, the presumed son of Theodoric III, as king.

THEODORIC IV DE CHELLES
713 - 720 - 737 A.D.

Son of Dagobert III, he governed under the control of Charles Martel who had removed him from Chelles Abbey where he had been brought up.

CHILDERIC III THE LAZY
714 - 743 - 753 A.D.

Son of Chilperic II, selected by Charles Martel as successor to Theodoric IV, he was crowned in 743 A.D. by Pepin the Short, mayor of the palace. Deposed by Pepin, he was confined to a monastery near Saint-Omer. His son was placed in St. Wandrille's Abbey.

The Carolingians

PEPIN THE SHORT
Jupille (Belgium) 715 - 743 - 753 A.D.
Queen: Bertha, known as Bertha of the Large Foot, 719 - 741 - 783

Pepin, one of the sons of Charles Martel and Rothrude, succeeded to the position of mayor of the palace in Paris which he held

jointly with his brother, Carloman, in 741 A.D. In 750, Pepin the Short obtained permission from Pope Zacharias to depose Childeric III.

He was then proclaimed king (751 A.D.) and was crowned in Soissons by St. Boniface (752). He fought the Duke of Aquitaine and the Saracen, and died after having shared out his kingdom between his two sons.

CHARLES I THE GREAT OR CHARLEMAGNE
(From the Latin Carolus Magnus)
742 - 768 - 814 A.D.
Queen: Hildegard, 758 - 771 - 783 A.D.

As the elder son of Pepin the Short and Bertha, he was crowned king in 751 A.D. and reigned initially over Neustria, Austrasia, and Western Aquitaine. In 771 A.D, he inherited his brother Carloman's possessions. Once he had re-restablished the unity of the «Regnum Francorum», Pope Leo III crowned him Holy Roman Emperor on Christmas Day in the year 800 A.D, in Rome.

During his reign, he pursued two main ambitions - the construction of a vast Christian empire in the Western world and the re-establishment of the Roman order. His territory stretched as far as the R. Elbe, making it even larger than the empire once ruled by Rome.

From his palace in Aix-la-Chapelle, he granted Counts and Bishops lands for which they were given direct responsibility. Their work was monitored by Charlemagne's missi dominici. In order to improve the effectiveness of his government, he replaced thitherto spoken orders by written instructions (capitulaires). He founded monasteries and schools, and was a patron of the Arts. He led countless military campaigns - in Lombardy (774 A.D.), against the Saxons who were defeated in 804 A.D, against the Arabs in Spain in 778 A.D, against the Bavarians, and against the Avars in Hungary (791 - 796 A.D.). The Act of Thionville (806 A.D) divided the Empire between his three sons, while he was still alive.

LOUIS I THE DEBONAIR OR THE PIOUS
Chasseneuil 778 - 814 - 840 A.D.
Queen: Judith of Bavaria, 800 - 819 - 845

Louis was one of Charlemagne and Hildegard's sons. When his brothers died, he was able to re-unite the entire Empire, in 814 A.D. In order to ensure his succession while

he was still alive, he divided the Empire into three kingdoms which he gifted, with primacy to the eldest, to his three sons (Ordinatio Imperii, 817 A.D.). When Judith, Louis the Pious' second wife, had another son, Charles, in 823 A.D, she demanded that he be given the same advantages as his brothers. This called into question the division of territory agreed to in 817 A.D. In the end, Charlemagne's vast empire was redivided (Treaty of Verdun, 843 A.D.) between Louis the German, Charles and Lothair.

CHARLES II THE BALD
Frankfurt 823 - 840 - Avrieux 877 A.D.
Queen: Ermentrude, ? - 842 - 869 A.D.
Charles was the son of Louis I the Pious and Judith of Bavaria. He held much of the Empire after having stood firm in the face of rivalry on the part of his half-brothers, Lothair, Pepin and Louis. After mounting the throne of France in 843 A.D, he was crowned Emperor of the Romans in 875 A.D.

LOUIS II THE STAMMERER
846 - 877 - Compiègne 879 A.D.
Queens: Ansgarde ? - 862 - ?
Adelaide ? - ? - ?
Louis was the son of Charles II the Bald and Ermentrude. He rebelled against his father and was grudgingly acknowledged king in 877 A.D. During his reign, the kingdom began to crumble away in a multiplicity of territories governed by noblemen.

LOUIS III and CARLOMAN
Louis: 863 - 879 - 882 A.D.
Carloman: 866 - 879 - 884 A.D.
Louis and his brother, who were the sons of Louis II the Stammerer and Ansgarde, reigned jointly. They fought the Vikings on the banks of the Loire and in Normandy. When Louis III died, Carloman reigned on his own.

CHARLES THE FAT
839 - 884 - 888 A.D.
Queen: Princess Richard of Scotland, ? - 877 - 894 A.D.
Charles, the son of Louis the German and grandson of Louis the Debonair, became King of France in 884 A.D. in preference to Charles the Simple. He was present at the Siege of Paris by the Vikings in 885 A.D. but made no attempt to put up any resistance. He withdrew to Alsace, was deposed at the Diet of Tribur (November 887 A.D.) and sought refuge in the monastery in Reichenau in Swabia where he died the following year.

EUDES
860 - 888 - 898
Queen Theoderade, ? - ? - ?
Eudes was the elder son of Robert the Strong and was Count of Paris, a town which he defended successfully during the Viking siege of 885 A.D despite the inertia of the reigning monarch. In 888 A.D, the country's leading noblemen crowned him King in Compiègne. This brought him into opposition with the Carolingian monarch, Charles the Simple, whom the Archbishop of Reims had already crowned in 893 A.D. After a confused period of conflict, Eudes, who was in poor health, entered negotiations with his opponent and died the following year, after having advised his vassals to recognise the legitimacy of Charles' claim.

CHARLES III THE SIMPLE
879 - 898 - 929 A.D.
Queen: Eadgifu of England, 896 - 917 - 951 A.D.
As the posthumous son of Louis II the Stammerer and Adelaide, Charles' rights to the throne were hotly contested. Crowned in Reims in 893 A.D, he then shared power with Eudes (from 896 to 898) before reigning on his own from 898 to 923 A.D. He negotiated peace with the Vikings (Treaty of Saint-Clair-sur-Epte, 911 A.D) and authorised their settlements in the Seine Valley. The legitimacy of his claim to the throne was contested by Duke Robert (brother of the dead King Eudes) who, after being crowned in Reims in 922 A.D, was attacked near Soissons by Charles III. Robert was killed; Charles was defeated and forced to flee. Later, Charles was ambushed in Château-Theodoric and imprisoned in Péronne. His wife left for England, taking with her their son, the future Louis IV from Overseas.

ROBERT I
860 - 922 - 923 A.D.
Queen: Beatrice of Vermandois, ? - 893 - ?
Robert, the second son of Robert the Strong, had his lands and titles confirmed by Charles the Simple who, in addition, granted

Jehan Roy des auc

him the sovereignty of Burgundy. He fought the Normans then rebelled aginst the king (920 A.D.). Crowned in Reims in 922 A.D, he was attacked near Soissons by Charles the Simple and killed. Charles was defeated and forced to flee.

RAOUL or RUDOLPH
? - 923 - Auxerre 936 A.D.
Queen: Emma, ? - ? - 935 A.D.

Rudolph was the son of Duke Richard of Aquitaine and the son-in-law of Duke Robert I of Burgundy. He succeeded his father-in-law with the consent of the latter's son, Hugh the Great.

He fought the Hungarians, Germans, and Normans and died childless.

LOUIS IV FROM OVERSEAS
918 - 936 - 954 A.D.
Queen: Gerberge of Saxony, 913 - 939 - 949 A.D.

After the defeat of his father, Charles the Simple, his mother, Eadgifu, took him to England, to the Court of his grandfather, Edward the Elder. After returning to France, Louis had to overcome the coalition led by Hugh the Great who wanted to reign in his place. Allied with King Otto I of Germany and King Conrad of Provence, he captured Reims. In 948 A.D, the Pope excommunicated Hugh and Louis' authority was re-established.

LOTHAIR
Reims 941 - 954 - Reims 986 A.D.
Queen: Emma, ? - ? - 989 A.D.

Lothair was the son of Louis IV and Gerberge of Saxony and, until he came of age, it was the Bishop of Cologne who governed the kingdom. Lothair's policies led to the invasion of Lorraine by Otto II but Lothair succeeded in repulsing the attack thanks to the help of Hugh Capet in 978 A.D. Otto II died in 983 A.D. Lothair then took advantage of the fact that Otto III was only three years old to try to destabilise the Holy German Empire.

LOUIS V THE DO-NOTHING
967 - 986 - Compiègne 987 A.D.
Queen: Adelaide of Anjou, ? - ? - ?

Lothair's son was crowned in 978 and was unfairly nicknamed «the Do-Nothing King».

He was laying siege to Reims in which Archbishop Adlabero was conspiring against him, when he died as a result of a hunting accident in Compiègne Forest. He had no heir and was succeeded on the throne by Hugh Capet.

The Capetians

HUGH CAPET
939 - 987 - 996 A.D.
Queen: Adelaide of Aquitaine, ? - 970 - 1004

Elder son of Hugh the Great, Count of Paris, he was elected to the throne and crowned in Noyon before being anointed in Reims (987 A.D.). He immediately made arrangements for his son Robert's accession to the throne. Duke Charles of Lorraine, the last of the Carolingian pretenders, struggled to regain the crown. He was taken prisoner and died in Orléans thereby ending all rivalry for Hugh Capet and his son.

However, Hugh Capet was only ever a feudal lord, with scarcely any more power than his vassals, and he was unable to prevent the kingdom crumbling further away.

ROBERT II THE PIOUS
972 - 996 - 1031
Queens: Bertha of Burgundy, 964 - 996 - 1024
Constance of Arles: ? - 1003 - 1032

Robert was the son of Hugh Capet and Adelaide of Aquitaine and was crowned in the year his father was anointed as King (987 A.D.). Pope Gregory V challenged his marriage with Bertha, who was a blood relation, and the Council of Rome ordered them to separate in 998 A.D. He remarried, this time with Constance, the daughter of the Count of Provence and Arles. He annexed Burgundy to the Crown (1002-1016) followed by the counties of Dreux (1015) and Melun (1016). He also assisted the monks of Cluny in the reform of their Order and severely repressed heresies which were beginning to come to the fore.

HENRY I
1008 - 1031 - Vitry-aux-Loges 1075
Queen: Anne of Kiev, 1024 - 1051 - 1075
Henry, the son of Robert II and

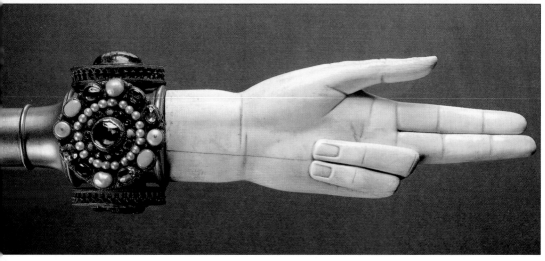

Constance of Provence, was anointed king in 1027. Shortly after his accession to the throne, he put down the rebellion of the lords of «Francia».

PHILIP I
1052 - 1060 - Melun 1108
Queen: Bertha of Holland, 1055 - 1072 - 1094
Philip, the son of Henry I and Anne of Kiev, was criticised by the Roman Catholic Church for his scandalous behaviour and detested by the population who were tired of his acts of highway robbery. In 1092, he repudiated his wife, Bertha, and kidnapped Bertrada de Montfort, the Count of Anjou's wife. A number of excommunications were heaped upon his head. His reign was marked by the First Crusade (1096), in which he took no part himself. On the other hand, he extended the royal estates to include the counties of Vermandois, Gâtinais and the French Vexin.

LOUIS VI THE FAT
Paris 1084 - 1108 - Paris 1137
Queen: Adelaide of Savoy, 1110 - 1115 - 1154
Louis, the son of Philip I and Bertha of Holland put an end to the disorder caused by pillaging noblemen in the Paris Basin and, for more than twenty years, he fought Thibaut IV of Champagne, a fearsome conspirator. He also attacked Henry I Beauclerc, King of England. He married his elder son, Louis, to Eleanor of Aquitaine. With Suger as his Minister, he confirmed the sovereignty of the monarch and enhanced the Crown properties.

LOUIS VII THE YOUNGER
Paris 1120 - 1137 - Paris 1180
Queens: Eleanor of Aquitaine, 1122 - 1137 - 1204
Constance of Castile, ? - 1154 - 1160
Alix of Champagne, ? - 1160 - 1206
Louis VII was the son of Louis VI and Adelaide of Savoy. He retained his father's ministers (including Suger who was Abbot of Saint-Denis) and put the finishing touches to policies aimed at the submission of the feudal lords in the Paris Basin. Two major events took place during his reign - his departure for the Second Crusade (1147-1149) and his divorce from Eleanor of Aquitaine in 1152.

She married Henry II, Count of Anjou, in 1154. He mounted the throne of England and owned an enclave in France that posed a threat to the nation (Normandy, Auvergne, Aquitaine, and Guyenne).

PHILIP II AUGUSTUS
Gonesse 1165 - 1180 - Mantes 1223
Queens: Isabella of Hainaut, 1170 - 1180 - 1190
Ingeborg of Denmark, 1176 - 1193 - 1236
Agnes of Meran, ? - 1196 - 1201
Philip, the son of Louis VII and Alix of Champagne, ordered cruel repression of the Jews who were held responsible for public disasters. He also put down a revolt by the country's noblemen. Then, in 1187, he began a war against the House of England, forcing Henry II to capitulate at Azay-le-Rideau in 1189. Philip II smashed an awesome coalition (England, Flanders, Germany) at Bouvines in 1214. He strengthened his power, extended the royal estates and, at the same time, gave them a well-structured organisation. He also took control of the feudal system, gained a hold on the temporal power of the Church, and embellished Paris, commissioning the building of new town walls, the first Louvre palace, Notre-Dame Cathedral and the University.

LOUIS VIII THE LION
Paris 1187 - 1223 - Montpensier 1226
Queen: Blanche of Castile, 1188 - 1200 - 1252
This son of Philip Augustus and Isabella of Hainaut became king in 1223. He led the crusade against the Albigensians, thereby paving the way for the annexation of the county of Toulouse.

LOUIS IX or St. LOUIS
Poissy 1214 - 1226 - Tunis 1270
Queen: Margaret of Provence, 1221 - 1234 - 1295
Louis was the son of Louis VIII and Blanche of Castile who governed the country as regent from 1226 to 1236. He successfully stood up to a dangerous coalition led by Hugh de Lusignan and Raymond VII of Toulouse with the backing of Henry III of England. During the Seventh Crusade (1248-1254), he captured Damietta but he was defeated at al-Mansurah in February 1250.

St. Louis b
El Greco, now
in the Louvr
(Louvre Museum, © R.M.

Despite the Pope's advice, the reticence of his lords, and his own poor health, he set off from Aigues-Mortes for the Eighth Crusade and died from plague during the Siege of Tunis. He was a diplomat, a dynamic man with an innate sense of justice and equity, who created the Parliament and kept a watchful eye on his bailiffs, seneschals and provosts. He founded a number of hospitals, including the «Quinze-Vingts» for three hundred knights whose eyes had been put out by the Saracen, and commissioned the building of the Sainte-Chapelle in Paris. He was canonised in 1297.

PHILIP III THE BOLD

Poissy 1245 - 1270 - Perpignan 1285

Queens: Isabella of Aragon, 1247 - 1262 - 1271

Marie de Brabant, 1254 - 1274 - 1321

Philip, the son of Louis IX and Margaret of Provence, was proclaimed king beneath the walls of Tunis. On the death of Alphonse of Poitiers, St. Louis' brother, he inherited Poitou, Auvergne, the Saintes area, and the Toulouse and Albi regions. He backed Charles of Anjou, King of Sicily, against Peter III of Aragon and led the «Aragon Crusade» during which he lost his fleet at Las Hormigas, in 1285.

PHILIP IV THE FAIR

Fontainebleau 1268 - 1285 - Fontainebleau 1314

Queen: Joan of Navarre, 1273 - 1284 - 1305

This son of Philip III and Isabella of Aragon showed enormous talent as an administrator and an extremely well-developed sense of foresight as regards foreign policy by putting an end to the Aragonese conflict begun by his father (Treaty of Agnani, 1295). He perfected existing institutions, strengthened the hold of the Chancellory, defined the functions of the Parliament, and reformed financial administration. However, in order to meet the grave economic difficulties that beset him, he had recourse to a number of risky expedients. He altered the coinage, persecuted the Lombards and Jews, and taxed Church property, which led to two serious conflicts i.e. the «Anagni Attack» in 1303 against Boniface VIII followed by the election of Clement V, the French Pope in Avignon, and the arrest of the Knights Templar in 1307 (including the confiscation of the Order's wealth and the torture of the Grand Master of the Temple, Jacques Molay, in 1314).

LOUIS X THE STUBBORN

Paris 1289 - 1314 - Vincennes 1316

Queens: Margaret of Burgundy, 1290 - 1305 - 1315

Clémence of Hungary, 1293 - 1315 - 1328

Louis, the elder son of Philip the Fair and Joan of Navarre, married Margaret of Burgundy in 1305. However, she was later accused of adultery and was strangled in her prison cell. He then married Clémence of Hungary. During his reign, which was marked by baronial discontent, he left his uncle, Charles of Valois, to govern the kingdom.

JOHN I THE POSTHUMOUS

Paris 1316 - 1316 - Paris 1316

This son of Louis X and Clémence of Hundary was born on 15th November 1316, five months after his father's death, and died on 19th November when he was only five days old. His uncle, Philip, Count of Poitou, who had been regent prior to his birth, was accused of having caused the infant's death in order to reign in his stead. He succeeded John under the title of Philip V in January 1317.

PHILIP V THE TALL

Paris 1292 - 1316 - Longchamps 1322

Queen: Joan of Burgundy, 1292 - 1307 - 1330

Philip was the second son of Philip IV the Fair and Joan of Navarre. He had acted as regent before the birth of John I and mounted the throne after his death, brushing aside the claim from his niece, Joan, despite the fact that she was older than he was. He was a remarkable administrator. He continued the policies first laid down by Philip the Fair, established the units of currency, weights and measures, organised the first Court of Accounts, and perfected the royal law courts. He also made Lille, Douai and Orchies part of the Crown domain.

CHARLES IV THE FAIR

Clermont 1294 - 1322 - Vincennes 1328

Queens: Blanche of Burgundy, 1296 - 1307 - 1326

Mary of Luxemburg, 1305 - 1322 - 1324
Joan of Evreux, ? - 1325 - 1371
Charles, the third son of Philip IV the Fair and Joan of Navarre, mounted the throne after the death of his brother, Philip, by virtue of the decision taken in 1316 which formally excluded women from succeeding to the Crown of France. During his reign, he maintained the pressure of the monarchy on the country's noblemen. He died childless and was the last direct descendent of the Capetians on the throne of France.

The Valois

PHILIP VI
1293 - 1328 - Nogent-le-Roi 1350
Queens: Jeanne de Bourbon, 1293 - 1313 - 1348
Blanche of Navarre, ? - 1349 - 1398
The reign of Philip, the son of Charles of Valois and Margaret of Sicily, began with the sombre One Hundred Years' War. At the same time, the country was in the grip of a serious economic crisis and was struck by the Black Death. Faced with financial difficulties, the king convened the States General (1346-1347) and instituted a new tax on salt. Despite the problems, the royal estates were extended to include Champagne, Brie, Montpellier and Dauphiné.

JOHN II THE GOOD
Orléans 1319 - 1350 - London 1364
Queens: Bonne of Luxemburg, 1316 - 1332 - 1349
Joan of Burgundy, 1326 - 1350 - 1361
John, the son of Philip VI and Jeanne de Bourbon, was criticised by the Provincial Estates because of his royal profligacy. Captured in Poitiers in 1356 after a conflict opposing him to Philip of Navarre (brother of Charles the Bad), he signed a treaty in London in 1359 that gave him his freedom in exchange for a huge ransom which was then refused by the States of Paris. His freedom was renegotiated prior to the signing of the Treaty of Brétigny in 1360. He returned to France, leaving behind as a hostage his son, the Duke of Anjou, who failed to keep his word and escaped. The king was therefore forced to return to London, where he died.

CHARLES V THE WISE
Vincennes 1338 - 1364 - Nogent 1380
Queen: Jeanne de Bourbon, 1338 - 1350 - 1377
Charles was the elder son of John II the Good and Bonne of Luxemburg. After the defeat at Poitiers in 1356, his father was held prisoner by the English and it was Charles who acted as regent, dealing with a political, economic and social situation that was nothing short of deplorable. He obtained his father's freedom through the Treaty of Brétigny in 1360. Assisted by du Guesclin, he imposed peace on Charles the Bad, wiped out the robber bands that were terrorising the country (the so-called «Grandes Compagnies») and pacified the nation as a whole (on his death, the English had lost all their French territories except Calais, Cherbourg, Brest, Bordeaux and Bayonne).

CHARLES VI THE MAD
Paris 1368 - 1380 - Paris 1422
Queen: Isabella of Bavaria, 1371 - 1385 - 1435
Charles, the elder son of Charles V and Jeanne de Bourbon, was unable to govern in any real sense of the word since power was firmly in the hands of his uncles until 1388 and he then went mad in 1392 (he died in the Saint-Pol Residence in 1422). In 1407, the Duke of Burgundy, John the Fearless, ordered the assassination of the Duke of Orléans who had declared himself regent, thereby starting a civil war between the Armagnac and Burgundian factions. Henry V of England took advantage of the situation and inflicted defeat upon the French at Azincourt (1415). John the Fearless was murdered during an attempt at reconciliation with the Armagnacs. The new Duke of Burgundy, Philip the Good, then signed the Treaty of Troyes (1420) with the English, which gave them the right to the French throne (Henry V, having married Charles V's daughter, was to become King of France when the French sovereign died).

CHARLES VII THE VICTORIOUS
Paris 1403 - 1422 - Mehun-sur-Yèvre 1461
Queen: Mary of Anjou, 1404 - 1422 - 1463
Charles, the son of Charles VI and Isabella of Bavaria, was only acknowledged

as King of France by the Armagnac faction, since Henry VI of England had been proclaimed King of France on the death of his father, Henry V, in 1422. Having sought refuge in Berry, the «little king of Bourges», who had no allies and was unable to take firm decisions, saw most of his kingdom subject to English rule. Joan of Arc liberated Orléans and had the king anointed in Reims (1429), thereby arousing a sense of nationalism in the country as a whole. This was the beginning of the systematic reconquest of the kingdom. Yet, in 1431, this did not prevent Charles VII from abandoning the woman who had saved him. He re-established the financial institutions and set them on a durable footing, modernised the army, relaunched economic activity and put down the Praguerie, a revolt by princes of the realm.

LOUIS XI
Bourges 1423 - 1461 - Plessis-lez-Tours 1483
Queens: Margaret of Scotland, ? - 1436 - 1445
Charlotte of Savoy, 1442 - 1457 - 1483
Louis, the son of Charles VII and Mary of Anjou, took part in the princes' revolt against his father but succeeded in regaining his confidence. He recaptured Dieppe from the English (1443) and took the County of Armagnac (1444) but then aroused his father's suspicions because of his intrigues and his open hostility towards Agnès Sorel. After mounting the throne in 1461, he dismissed his father's counsellors and attempted to break the power of the nobility. When Charles the Bold died (1477), he annexed Burgundy and Picardy to the Crown and extended the kingdom by the addition of Anjou (1480), Maine and Provence (1481), and Cerdagne and Roussillon. Feared for his excessive severity (he imprisoned Cardinal La Ballue, and had the Count of Armagnac and Constable de Saint-Paul executed), he nevertheless made some remarkable achievements. By setting up the post office, re-establishing law and order in the kingdom and making the roads safer to travel on, he encouraged trade and industry.

CHARLES VIII THE AFFABLE
Amboise 1470 - 1483 - Amboise 1498

Queen: Anne of Brittany 1477 - 1491 - 1514
Charles, the son of Louis XI and Charlotte of Savoy, married the heiress to Brittany in 1491, thereby annexing the province to the Crown. He claimed hypothetical rights to the Crown of Naples and led his first military campaign in Italy in 1495 where the French discovered a civilisation that was refined and intellectually brilliant. He was planning a second trans-Alpine expedition when he died, having struck his head on the lintel of a particularly low door in Amboise Castle (1498).

LOUIS XII, THE FATHER OF THE PEOPLE
Blois 1462 - 1498 - Paris 1515
Queens: Jeanne of Valois, 1464 - 1476 - 1505
Anne of Brittany, 1477 - 1499 - 1514
Mary Tudor, ? - 1514 - 1533
Louis, the son of Mary of Cleves and Charles d'Orléans, was subjected to a strict upbringing by Louis XI whose sickly daughter, Jeanne, he married. When Charles VIII died without an heir, Louis succeeded him and had his marriage with Jeanne annulled so that he could marry Anne of Brittany, thereby bringing the province back to the Crown. He took part in Charles VIII's first trans-Alpine expedition and ordered the second Italian campaign (1498-1515). Louis XII improved the administration of justice, helped to instigate a healthy economy and strengthened royal authority.

In the field of the Arts, the French were subject to a very strong Italian influence. This period was marked by the blossoming of the Renaissance in France.

FRANCIS I
Cognac 1494 - 1515 - Rambouillet 1547
Queens: Claude of France, 1499 - 1514 - 1524
Eleanor of Austria, 1498 - 1530 - 1558
Francis, the son of Charles of Angoulême and Louise of Savoy, succeeded his cousin and father-in-law, Louis XII, who died without leaving a male heir. As soon as he mounted the throne, he continued to work towards achieving his predecessors' dream i.e. the conquest of the Milan and Naples areas. He defeated the Swiss at Marignano (1515). Elected Holy Germany Emperor in 1519,

Portrait of Charle
VII by Fouque
now in the Louvre
(Louvre Museum, © R.M.I

Charles V posed a threat to France. Despite seeking an alliance with England (the Field of the Cloth of Gold, 1520), Francis I signed the Treaty of Madrid after his defeat at Pavia (1525). In order to remove the dishonour of defeat, Francis, the «Most Christian King», allied himself with Soliman the Magnificent and forced Charles V to accept the Treaty of Cambrai. During his reign he strengthened the absolute character of the monarchy and, as patron of the Arts, encouraged the spread of the Renaissance style. He also founded the Collège de France.

HENRY II
Saint-Germain-en-Laye 1519 - 1547 - Paris 1559

Queen: Catherine de Médicis, 1519 - 1533 - 1589

Henry, the second son of Francis I and Claude of France, became heir to the throne when his brother, the Dauphin Francis, died in 1536. Influenced by his mother, his mistress Diane de Poitiers, the de Guise faction, and de Coligny, he continued to implement the main policies launched by his father, fought the English, and forced Charles V to abdicate in 1556 after a period of conflict. It was during his reign that the terrible Wars of Religion began. He died of wounds inflicted on him during a tournament by Montgomery, Captain of his Guard. The joust had been organised to celebrate the marriage of his daughter Elisabeth to Philip II of Spain.

FRANCIS II
Paris 1544 - 1559 - Orléans 1560

Queen: Mary Stuart, Queen of Scots, 1542 - 1558 - 1587

The elder son of Henry II and Catherine de Médicis handed over all his power to the Duke de Guise and the Cardinal of Lorraine who persecuted the Protestants and put down the Amboise conspiracy. He was in constant poor health and he died childless, abandoning the country to a civil war opposing the Guises and Bourbons.

CHARLES IX
Saint-Germain 1550 - 1560 - Vincennes 1574

Queen: Elisabeth of Austria, 1555 - 1570 - 1592

Charles, second son of Henry II and Catherine de Médicis, was dominated by his mother. His reign was marked by the Wars of Religion opposing Catholics and Protestants. Catherine de Médicis and Michel de l'Hospital sought in vain to establish religious conciliation (Colloquy of Poissy in 1561 and Edict of January 1562) and they granted freedom to the Protestants to worship as they pleased. This was followed by a violent backlash leading up to the St. Bartholomew's Day Massacre (24th August 1572) during which Catherine de Médicis had the Protestants' leader, Admiral Coligny, murdered.

HENRY III
Fontainebleau 1551 - 1574 - Saint-Cloud 1589

The third son of Henry II was King of Poland and did not return to France until the death of his brother, Charles IX. He quickly lost favour because of his extravagance. The Wars of Religion continued during his reign, opposing the Protestants (supported by England and Denmark) and Roman Catholics (supported by Spain). The conflict was made worse by political and dynastic rivalries since, on Henry III's death, the Crown should by right have passed to Henry of Navarre, leader of the Huguenots. Threatened by the Catholic League and the de Guise faction, Henry III ordered the murder of the Duke de Guise in Blois (1588). He recognised Henry of Navarre as his rightful successor and was stabbed to death on 2nd August 1589 by a Jacobin friar named Jacques Clément.

The Bourbons

HENRY IV
Pau 1553 - 1589 - Paris 1610

Queens: Margaret of Valois, 1553 - 1572 - 1615

Marie de Médicis, 1573 - 1600 - 1642

Henry, the son of Antoine de Bourbon and Jeanne d'Albret, was, on the death of Henry III, the closest in line to Hugh Capet. Assisted by Sully, he was admirably successful in pulling out of the doldrums a kingdom exhausted by war. He subdued the feudal lords, put the country's finances on a more stable footing, encouraged farming and promoted trade. Since the Catholic League refused to

Henry II by Clouet
Henry III
Quesnel
and Henry IV
Pourbus
These three
portraits are
in the Louvre
(Louvre Museum, © R.M.)

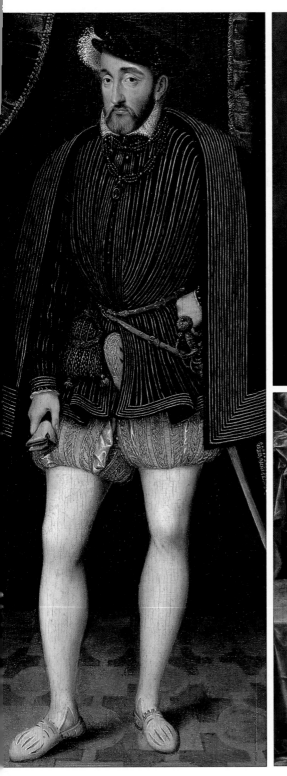

acknowledge his right to the throne when Henry III died, he had to reconquer power. His conversion to Roman Catholicism (1593) followed by his coronation in Chartres, the submission of Paris (1594) and the capture of Amiens (1596) were the main features in this conquest. The Edict of Nantes (1598) marked the end of the civil war and the peace treaty signed in Vervins ended the wars with foreign countries. After a short war against the Duke of Savoy, he annexed Bresse, Bugey and the Gex area to the kingdom. He was murdered by Ravaillac.

LOUIS XIII THE JUST

Fontainebleau 1601 - 1610 - Saint-Germain 1643

Queen: Anne of Austria, 1601 - 1615 - 1666

Louis was the eldest son of Henry IV and Marie de Médicis. His mother acted as regent jointly with Concini until 1617, thereby excluding her son from government. Encouraged by de Luynes to whom he had granted wide-ranging powers, Louis had Concini assassinated in 1617. The king then remained loyal to Richelieu, who became his principal minister in 1624 and, on his adviser's death in 1642, he appointed Mazarin to replace him, on Richelieu's recommendation. Together, they re-established royal authority, substituting an administrative structure based on the monarch's power. They also developed trade and industry. The main events in his reign were the Siege of La Rochelle (a Protestant stronghold) in 1628, the Peace Treaty of Alès (1629) which granted the Protestants freedom of conscience, the Cinq-Mars Conspiracy (1642) and the conquest of the Roussillon.

LOUIS XIV THE GREAT

Saint-Germain 1638 - 1643 - Versailles 1715

Queen: Maria Teresa of Austria, 1638 - 1660 - 1683

The childhood and adolescence of Louis XIII and Anne of Austria's son were marked by the Fronde Revolt (1648-1652). This left him excessively wary of the royal law courts and determined to establish an absolute monarchy. It was Mazarin who governed the kingdom until 1661, with the agreement of the King who had achieved his legal majori-ty in 1651. Louis XIV began his own reign in 1661 and, surrounded by a number of remarkable counsellors (Colbert, Louvois, Vauban, Turenne etc.) remained an absolute monarch.

His reign was marked by four major wars i.e. The War of Devolution which ended in the Peace Treaty signed in Aix-la-Chapelle in 1668, the Franco-Dutch War (1672-1678) in reaction against the Triple Alliance between England, Holland and Sweden which ended with the Peace Treaty of Nijmegen in 1678, the War of the League of Augsburg of which the main outcome was the Revocation of the Edict of Nantes, and the War of Spanish Succession which ended in the Treaty of Utrecht (1713). Despite the religious strife that was such a feature of his reign, Louis XIV, a patron of the Arts, literature and science, encouraged industry, then in its infancy, and trade. He commissioned the palace of Versailles which was to reflect the «Age of Enlightenment» throughout Europe. This was where he «domesticated» his Court.

LOUIS XV THE BELOVED

Versailles 1710 - 1715 - Versailles 1774

Queen: Marie Leszczynska, 1703 - 1725 - 1768

Louis, the son of Louis of Burgundy and Marie-Adelaide of Savoy, succeeded his great-grandfather, Louis XIV. It is usual to distinguish six major periods in his reign. The years 1715-1726 were the years of the Duke d'Orléans' regency followed, despite the fact that the king had attained his legal majority, by the Duke of Bourbon's regency (Law's disastrous financial experiment, a break-off of relations with Spain whose Infanta had been sent back home despite being engaged to the king). Between 1726 and 1743, the country was governed by Cardinal Fleury (the budget was balanced for the first time since 1642), the king supported his father-in-law, Stanislas Leszczynski (War of the Polish Succession). The years 1740-1748 were marked by the War of the Austrian Succession and 1748-1763 by the Seven Years' War (1756-1763) which resulted in the loss of Canada and India. From 1763 to 1770, Choiseul did his best to provide the kingdom with some sort of economic recovery. France purchased Corsica, which the

English had coveted for its strategic position as a place from which to control the surrounding coastlines. Finally, from 1770 to 1774, Louis XV was under the influence of successive mistresses (Marquise de Pompadour, Duchess du Barry etc.). Choiseul was disgraced, the royal coffers were emptied, and royalty itself fell into disrepute.

LOUIS XVI

Versailles 1754 - 1774 - Paris 1793

Queen: Marie-Antoinette of Austria, 1755 - 1770 - 1793

Louis, son of the Dauphin Louis and Maria-Josepha of Saxony, and Louis XV's grandson, was unable to impose the reforms he wanted and he failed to support his ministers (Malesherbes, Turgot, Necker etc.) despite their competence. An economic crisis, worsened by the War of American Independence, led the government to convene the States General (5th May 1789). Badly advised and unable to free himself of the queen's influence, Louis XVI led the monarchy to its downfall. On 10th August 1792, the capture of the Tuileries palace marked the end of pre-revolutionary France. Incarcerated in the Temple with his family, the king was sentenced to death by a small majority and mounted the scaffold on 21st January 1793. His execution led to a powerful European coalition against France.

LOUIS XVIII

Versailles 1755 - 1814 - Paris 1824

Queen: Louise of Savoy, 1753 - 1771 - 1810

Louis XVIII, brother of Louis XVI, sought refuge in Koblenz in 1791 before moving to Italy, Russia and England. He returned to the throne of France after the coalition armies had defeated Napoleon in 1814. Proclaimed King of France, he resigned himself to accepting the constitutional regime set out in the Charter but was confronted by reactionaries in his entour-

age. He sought refuge in Ghent during the «One Hundred Days» and remounted the throne after Bonaparte's defeat at the Battle of Waterloo (18th June 1815).

CHARLES X

Versailles 1757 - 1824 - Goritz 1836

Queen: Marie-Thérèse of Sardinia, 1756 - 1773 - 1805

Charles, youngest son of the Dauphin Louis and Maria-Josepha of Saxony, and Louis XV's grandson, was the leader of the Ultras who promoted the concept of a return to the pre-Revolutionary regime. He became king on the death of his brother, Louis XVIII, and was crowned in Reims but he was forced to accept a more liberal political regime. He nevertheless signed four ordinances on 25th July 1830 dissolving the mainly liberal Chamber, modifying the Charter, and suppressing the freedom of the press. By doing so, he started the July Revolution (27th, 28th, 29th July) and had to abdicate on 2nd August.

LOUIS PHILIPPE I

Paris 1773 - 1830 - Claremont 1850

Queen: Marie-Amélie of the Sicilian Bourbons, 1782 - 1809 - 1886

Louis, son of the Duke d'Orléans also known as «Philippe-Egalité» (he had voted in favour of the death of his cousin, Louis XVI) and Adelaide de Bourbon-Penthièvre, was manoeuvred onto the throne by Lafayette and Laffite, the well-known banker. Between 1830 and 1840, he was faced with attempted revolts on the part of Legitimists (right-wing monarchist extremists) and Republicans but succeeded in steering a precarious middle course. In 1840, he handed power over to Guizot who governed the country for seven years. Louis refused to grant the people the reforms that they were demanding (including universal suffrage). This led to deep-seated discontent and to the 1848 uprising. He abdicated on 24th February 1848 and took refuge in England where he died.

Front cove
**Bust-reliquary o
St. Loui:
part of th
Notre-Dam
Cathedral treasure
Pari:**
(Photo by Gérard Boula)

Inse
**Crown-reliquar
of St. Loui:
now in the Louvr
Museum**
(Louvre Museum, © R.M.N

Back cove
**Charles .
by Gérar
now in the Palac
of Versaille**
(Palace of Versailles,
R.M.N

© 1995 - Édilarge S.A. - Éditions Ouest-France, Rennes
I.S.B.N. : 2.7373.1709.6 - Dépôt légal : janvier 1995 - N° d'éditeur : 3130.06.03.12.99
Imprimerie Raynard, La Guerche-de-Bretagne (35)